UNIQUE HEALTH IDENTIFIER ASSESSMENT TOOL KIT

MAY 2018

ADB

ASIAN DEVELOPMENT BANK

© 2018 Asian Development Bank
6 ADB Avenue, Mandaluyong City, 1550 Metro Manila, Philippines
Tel +63 2 632 4444; Fax +63 2 636 2444
www.adb.org

Some rights reserved. Published in 2018.

ISBN 978-92-9261-164-4 (print), 978-92-9261-165-1 (electronic)
Publication Stock No. TIM168320-2
DOI: http://dx.doi.org/10.22617/TIM168320-2

The views expressed in this publication are those of the authors and do not necessarily reflect the views and policies of the Asian Development Bank (ADB) or its Board of Governors or the governments they represent.

ADB does not guarantee the accuracy of the data included in this publication and accepts no responsibility for any consequence of their use. The mention of specific companies or products of manufacturers does not imply that they are endorsed or recommended by ADB in preference to others of a similar nature that are not mentioned.

By making any designation of or reference to a particular territory or geographic area, or by using the term "country" in this document, ADB does not intend to make any judgments as to the legal or other status of any territory or area.

Notes:
In this publication, "$" refers to United States dollars.
Corrigenda to ADB publications may be found at http://www.adb.org/publications/corrigenda.

CONTENTS

ACKNOWLEDGMENTS

The development of the *Unique Health Identifier Assessment Tool Kit* was led by the consultant Michael Stahl and Asian Development Bank staff Kirthi Ramesh and Susann Roth. The document was developed in close consultation with Lori Thorell (UNICEF) who provided support and input to developing this tool kit. The team is also grateful to Mia Harbitz for the valuable comments she provided. We thank all contributors for making this document practical and useful.

ABBREVIATIONS

CRVS   -   civil registration and vital statistics

HIV   -   human immunodeficiency virus

ICT   -   information and communication technology

SDG   -   Sustainable Development Goal

WHO   -   World Health Organization

INTRODUCTION

DO YOU
WANT TO
UNDERSTAND
how identifiers relevant for the health sector are currently being used in your country?

?

THIS TOOL KIT IS FOR YOU.

Using a modular series of easy-to-use questionnaires, this tool kit can help you:

- get an overview of the current use of identifiers important for the health sector,
- find opportunities to link existing patient identifiers,
- understand the existing legal framework and institutional setting for identification, and
- map the current stakeholders using identifiers relevant for health.

WHY
UNIQUE HEALTH IDENTIFIERS MATTER

Unique health identifiers are important for improving quality and continuum of care, strengthening surveillance of communicable diseases, eradicating diseases, and optimizing provider and payer transactions in health financing schemes.

When they can be uniquely identified, wherever and whenever they interact with different health service providers, patients have a better chance to experience continuity of care. Unique patient identification helps the health system to deliver better care, because the patients' unique health identifier can help attribute medical records across different providers to an individual subject of care. For health insurers, unique health identifiers can facilitate smoother payment systems, leading to faster claims reimbursements.

A unique identifier—usually a numeric or alphanumeric sequence ideally linked with biometric information—is necessary because other personal attributes to identify an individual such as name, date of birth, and gender can lead to duplications. Furthermore, these are often captured in different ways by different health care providers. Unique health identifiers, captured, for example, in a health client registry, are an important component of the overall enterprise architecture and can support strengthening information exchange.[1]

---

[1]   A health client registry is the central repository to which every player in the health sector should be able to connect. It stores a unique personal health identifier for every person who receives a health care service in a country. It contains patient demographics, e.g., name, date of birth, gender, and address. A health client registry can include individuals who are not eligible for inclusion in a citizen ID registry such as landed immigrants and refugees.

Proper health identity management also supports broader aims: once every service user can be properly identified, it becomes easier to achieve universal health coverage and measure progress toward the targets of the Sustainable Development Goal for health (SDG 3).

Malaria elimination is a prime example of the crucial role that unique health identifiers play in health care. To eliminate malaria, every malaria case must be rapidly diagnosed, treated, tracked, and investigated. This requires integrated registration systems and unique identifiers as well as interconnectivity and back-office capacity to handle secure and trustworthy identification systems that protect privacy and prevent unauthorized access to health information.

A more detailed discussion of the arguments for unique identifiers can be found in the Asian Development Bank policy brief: *On The Road To Universal Health Coverage: Every Person Matters: Unique Identifiers for Every Citizen Are Key to an Effective and Equitable Health System.*[2]

---

[2] ADB. 2016. On The Road to Universal Health Coverage: Every Person Matters. *ADB Briefs* No. 56. Manila. https://www.adb.org/sites/default/files/publication/183512/uhc-every-person-matters.pdf.

The Asian Development Bank Unique Health Identifier Assessment Tool Kit

The Asian Development Bank (ADB) conducted a mapping of patient identification methods used in Cambodia, the Lao People's Democratic Republic, and Myanmar. It revealed the complexity and fragmentation of identifiers used in the health sector. Health care organizations, integrated delivery systems, insurance companies, public programs, clinics, hospitals, physicians, and pharmacies often use their own patient identifiers, while the delivery and administration of health care frequently crosses organizational boundaries.

It became clear that a tool kit for health policymakers and implementers would be of value to better understand the situation before technical solutions could be designed and a road map developed to introduce unique health identifiers with the objective of improving service delivery. In particular, managers of programs tackling single diseases, such as malaria, tuberculosis, and HIV, expressed an urgent need to shift from aggregated patient data to individual patient records, which enable disease tracking in vulnerable populations, who often have no national ID.

With a clear picture of the current landscape, it becomes possible to move toward linking and harmonizing fragmented identifiers and patient records through a unique health identifier. By doing so, both delivery and administration of health care can be streamlined, quality of care improved, and administrative costs reduced.

The tool kit complements other identity management tool kits as it specifically focuses on the health sector. The Digital Identity Toolkit: A Guide for Stakeholders in Africa focuses mainly on foundational identity systems and is not specific to any sector.[3] Recently, the World Bank has published guidelines for ID4D (Identity for Development) diagnostics to evaluate a current and/or planned identity ecosystem.[4] The Inter-Agency Social Protection Assessments Partnership has further developed a tool that allows assessing identification systems for social protection.[5] Furthermore, the World Health Organization (WHO) has developed a rapid assessment of national civil registration and vital statistics systems.[6]

---

[3] World Bank Group. 2014. *Digital Identity Toolkit : A Guide for Stakeholders in Africa.* Washington, D.C.: World Bank.

[4] World Bank. 2018. *Guidelines for ID4D Diagnostics.* Washington, D.C.: World Bank.

[5] Inter Agency Social Assessments Partnership. 2016. *Identification Systems for Social Protection.* Washington, D.C.: World Bank.

[6] WHO. 2010. *Rapid assessment of national civil registration and vital statistics systems.* Geneva: WHO.

Figure 1: Paving the Way Toward a Unique Health Identifier

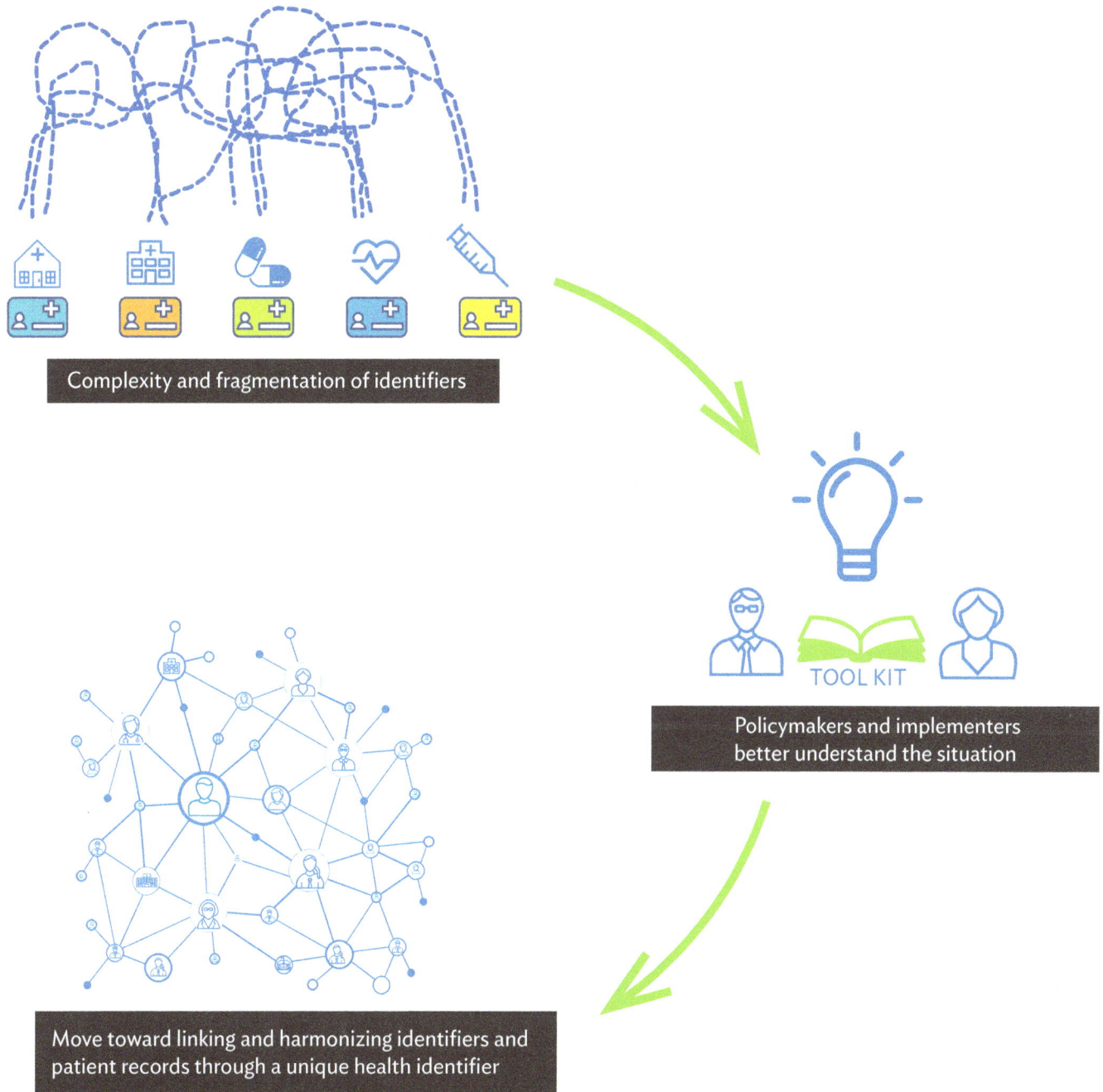

Complexity and fragmentation of identifiers

TOOL KIT

Policymakers and implementers better understand the situation

Move toward linking and harmonizing identifiers and patient records through a unique health identifier

Source: Authors.

HOW THE TOOL KIT WORKS

The tool kit is a compilation of questionnaires that can be selected according to a country's requirements. The questionnaires are not exhaustive but provide comprehensive guidance. The tool kit has a number of unique features.

1) THE TOOL KIT FOLLOWS A DRAWER APPROACH

The questionnaires in this mapping tool are divided into three broad sections (Figure 2):

1. legal, institutional, and political framework for identification, especially data privacy and confidentiality;
2. information and communication technology (ICT) infrastructure to support health and health sector-related registration and identification systems;[7]

3. available health and health sector-related registration and identification systems.

Within each of these three sections are several questionnaires that can be applied in a flexible manner depending on the interviewer's interests and focus, and the expertise of the respondent to be interviewed. Each of these questionnaires can be applied individually or in combination. It is recommended to apply the main questionnaires at a minimum (Figure 3).

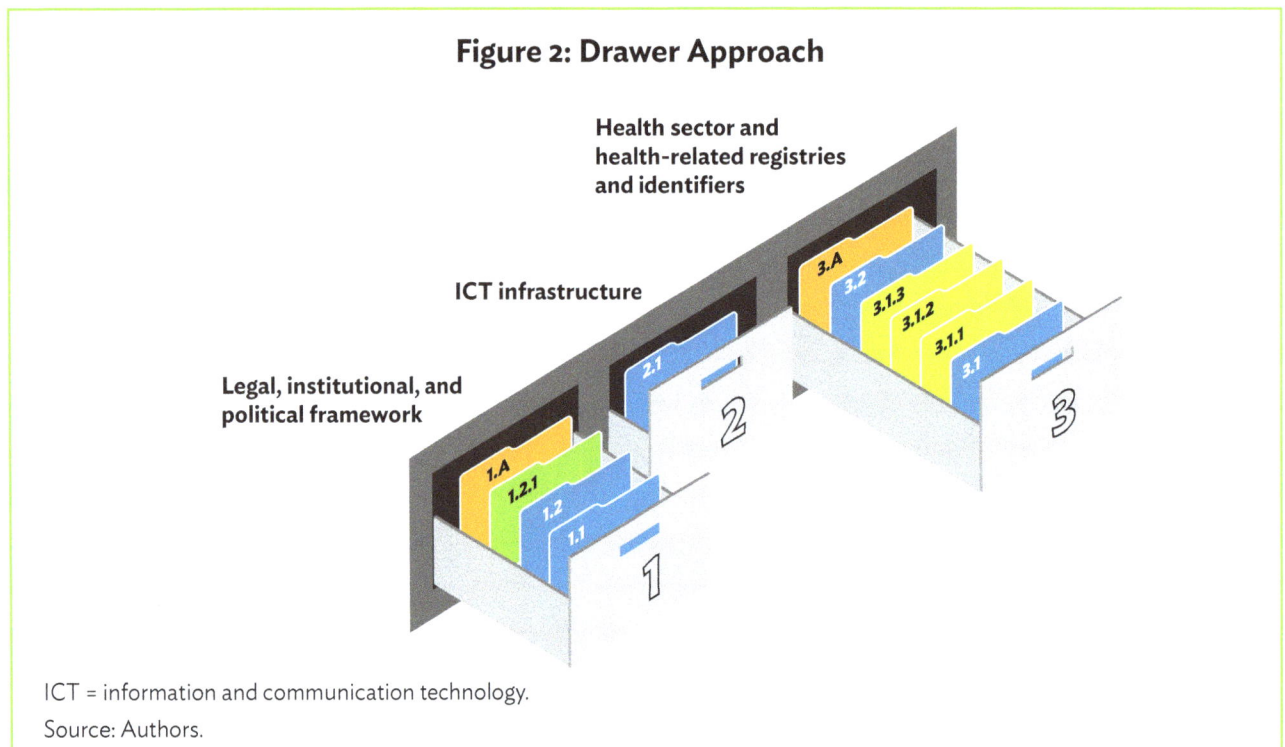

Figure 2: Drawer Approach

ICT = information and communication technology.
Source: Authors.

---

[7] Registries here refer to those that capture information about an individual and particular individuals seeking or potentially seeking health care services. Other registries in the health sector such as facility registries and health worker registries are not covered here.

Figure 3: Structure of the Tool Kit

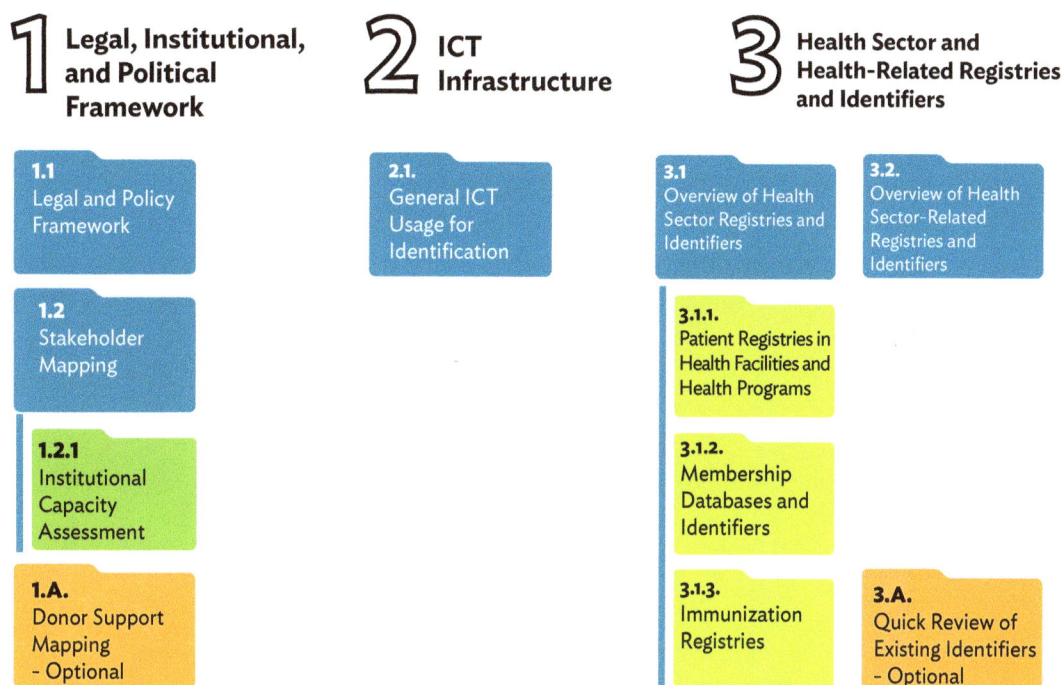

1 Legal, Institutional, and Political Framework

2 ICT Infrastructure

3 Health Sector and Health-Related Registries and Identifiers

1.1 Legal and Policy Framework

1.2 Stakeholder Mapping

1.2.1 Institutional Capacity Assessment

1.A. Donor Support Mapping - Optional

2.1. General ICT Usage for Identification

3.1 Overview of Health Sector Registries and Identifiers

3.2. Overview of Health Sector-Related Registries and Identifiers

3.1.1. Patient Registries in Health Facilities and Health Programs

3.1.2. Membership Databases and Identifiers

3.1.3. Immunization Registries

3.A. Quick Review of Existing Identifiers - Optional

ICT = information and communication technology.

Main Questionnaires

The blue folders are the main questionnaires recommended as a minimum to assess the situation in a country when considering introducing a unique health identifier.

For Detail on a Particular Institution

The dark green folder is a questionnaire that allows assessing the institutional capacity of a particular institution. It can be duplicated as often as necessary to be applied to the different institutions identified in the stakeholder mapping.

For Detail on Particular Registry and/or Identifier

The light green folders are questionnaires that allow assessing a particular registry and identifier in more detail. This approach accounts for the multiplicity of registries and identifiers that typically exist within the health sector: These questionnaires can be duplicated as often as necessary to be applied to the different registries and/or identifiers.

Optional

The orange folders are optional questionnaires. They can help map relevant donor support and perform a quick scan of available identification numbers within and beyond the health sector.

Source: Authors.

The tool kit can help users understand

- the existing legal framework for identification,
- stakeholders using different health and health sector-related registries and identifiers,
- digital technology usage for identification and registration,
- the multitude of existing health and health sector-related registries and identifiers, and
- whether centralized databases exist and whether patients are covered nationwide.

2) THE TOOL KIT COVERS HEALTH SECTOR AND HEALTH SECTOR-RELATED REGISTRIES AND IDENTIFIERS

Within the health sector, different providers and health system implementers may be using a variety of registries and record systems containing identifiers that are not necessarily unique. These may include patient identifiers at particular facilities or network of facilities; identifiers for a particular disease program or membership identification numbers of health insurance schemes. Membership identification of other social protection schemes are also included here.

At the same time there are several registration and identification systems outside the health sector that contribute to establishing a person's identity such as birth registries and national identification systems. These may also directly or indirectly support citizens to receive health care services.

The tool kit considers both identification and registration systems within and beyond the health sector, to understand the entire landscape of currently available registries and identifiers that could potentially be used for health purposes or linked with a planned unique health identifier.

Where applicable the questionnaires are therefore divided into three broad sections:

- health-specific
- health-related
- crosscutting

(h) Health-specific

Health sector registries and identifiers include:
- patient registries and identifiers (e.g., of particular health program; at a health facility or cluster of facilities; or for single disease programs, e.g., HIV, malaria, or tuberculosis)
- membership identification numbers for health insurance schemes and other social protection schemes

(hr) Health-related

Health sector-related registries and identifiers include:
- national ID numbers
- civil registration and vital statistics (CRVS) system

(c) Crosscutting

Crosscutting issues
- understanding the extent of cross-matching between identifiers
- covers topics that concern health sector and health sector-related registries and identifiers

3) THE TOOL KIT IS FOR VARIOUS USERS AND INTERVIEW PARTNERS

──────────────── The tool can be used by ────────────────

Government stakeholders who want to get an overview of existing identifiers relevant for the health sector in their country.

Experts who have a sound background in identification in the health sector.

System architects who want to get an overview and guidance for developing digital solutions to improve interoperability in the health sector.

Program managers in international organizations providing technical support in the health sector.

Recommended interview partners

The drawer approach allows different questionnaires (or selected questions) to be used for different respondents depending on their areas of expertise. Recommended respondents include staff in the

- Ministry of Health, Department of Planning/ Department of Information and Communication Technology;
- relevant ministry for the implementation of the CRVS system;
- relevant ministry or agency for the implementation of the national ID system (citizen ID);
- national hospitals;
- referral, provincial, and district hospitals;
- rural health centers;
- vertical disease program implementers (e.g., HIV, malaria, and tuberculosis);
- public health insurance funds (member registration division and information technology division);
- formal sector health insurers, community-based social health insurers, and health insurers for the poor, and for civil servants;
- pension funds and accident insurance funds;
- project managers of national and international development organizations; and/or
- immunization programs.

HOW TO
ORGANIZE MEETINGS WITH RESPONDENTS

Timely arrangement of interviews is a key success factor. The meeting request letter should highlight the purpose of a status quo analysis rather than propose specific software solutions. Government officials could seek support from consultants who have experience with identification mechanisms in the health sector.

Interviewers can fill out the questionnaires as far as possible by screening relevant literature, calling relevant respondents, or sending the selected questionnaires to development partners (e.g., send stakeholder mapping to map institutions) before the interview.

Experience shows that using Module 1.2 (Stakeholder mapping) and Module 3.1. (Overview of health sector registries and identifiers) is a good starting point for the tool kit user, particularly in countries with a highly fragmented health sector. Knowing which stakeholders are involved in which area of identifying a person will make it easier to select the right questionnaire during the interviews.

Providing respondents with the questionnaire in advance (e.g., by email) can help to establish trust because it reassures the respondents of the purpose of the interview, and allays fears that the motive is to elicit sensitive data or sell a particular product or software.

Experience shows that using Module 1.2 (Stakeholder Mapping) is a good starting point for the tool kit user, particularly in countries with a highly fragmented health sector.

During stakeholder visits, program managers should be available to explain the strategic approach of their particular work area. People who also know the business processes, as well as ICT staff who can explain the technical background of their databases and data structure (e.g., data format, online availability, ID number algorithms) should also be easily available. During interviews, it is helpful to clarify terms before asking further questions. Key terms have been explained in footnotes.

The assessment results should be presented in a stakeholder consultation workshop. It will generate more innovative ideas, can reveal political constraints, and help identify possible areas for collaboration.

The tool kit should preferably not be used in a multistakeholder meeting. Experience shows that some persons are less likely to share relevant information if people from other institutions are in the room.

PUTTING IT
ALL TOGETHER

A report discussing and explaining results from the analysis and overall assessment should be produced. The report may include a summary and discussion of existing registries and identifiers relevant for health. Other conditions existing in the country to introduce unique health identifiers can be discussed along the areas suggested in Figure 4. The conclusion could discuss gaps identified, and recommendations on how to address these.[8]

Figure 4: Assessing Existing Conditions to Introduce a Unique Health Identifier

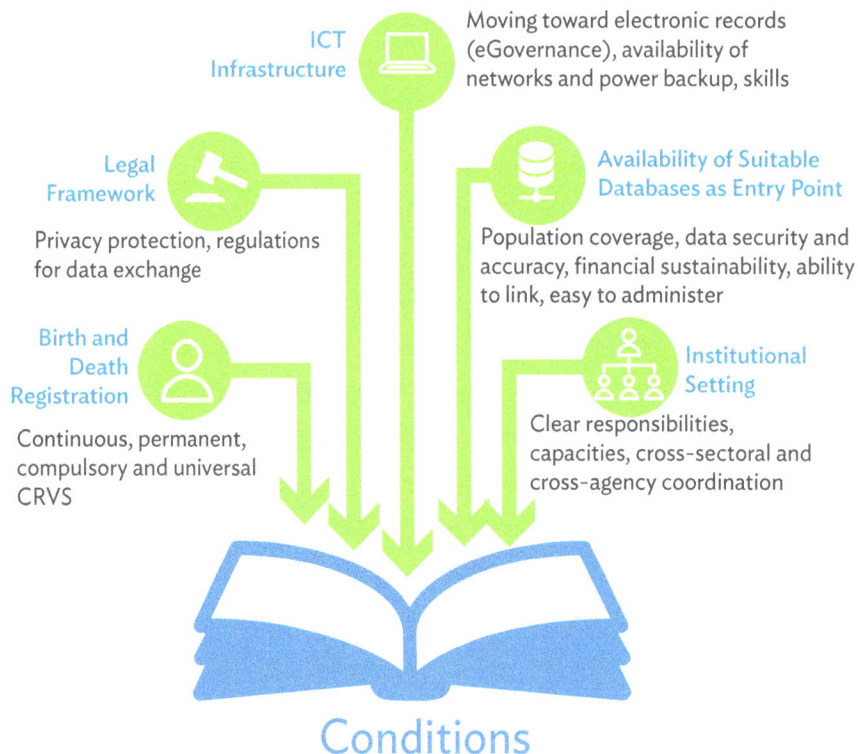

ICT Infrastructure
Moving toward electronic records (eGovernance), availability of networks and power backup, skills

Legal Framework
Privacy protection, regulations for data exchange

Availability of Suitable Databases as Entry Point
Population coverage, data security and accuracy, financial sustainability, ability to link, easy to administer

Birth and Death Registration
Continuous, permanent, compulsory and universal CRVS

Institutional Setting
Clear responsibilities, capacities, cross-sectoral and cross-agency coordination

Conditions

CRVS = civil registration and vital statistics, ICT = information and communication technology.
Source: Authors.

---

8   A set of shared principles endorsed by several organizations can further serve as a basis to assess existing or planned identification systems. World Bank Group and Center for Global Development. 2017. *Principles on Identification for Sustainable Development: Toward the Digital Age.*

As the tool kit aims to capture the status quo of existing identifiers and available registries in a particular country, the results of the questionnaire and the analysis should inform the discussion between relevant government stakeholders about gaps, policy options, and recommendations, as well as next steps to introduce identifiers for health purposes.

As conditions for introducing a unique health identifier will differ from country to country, the choice of the technical design as well as the prioritization of next steps will likewise vary. While some countries may be advanced in terms of their legal framework, they may not have sufficient ICT infrastructure in place. Other countries may have a comprehensive and robust population database in place that may serve as an entry point to build a patient registry, but may lack a robust legal framework. This tool kit will help determine existing conditions and help to identify opportunities and gaps, which in turn can inform next steps for each country, considering their current capacities.

The next steps will also have to be informed by the technical design the country chooses to introduce a unique health identifier. Some countries may choose to establish a completely new system for patient identification while others may choose to build on existing registries and identifiers. Where a robust and inclusive national identification system is in place, countries may opt to use this foundational ID for the health sector. Other countries may prefer to establish a separate unique health identifier used solely for the health sector.[9,10] It is beyond the scope of this tool kit to discuss different policy options for a unique health identifier. There is no blueprint in establishing a unique health identifier.

As conditions for introducing a unique health identifier will differ from country to country, the choice of the technical design as well as the prioritization of next steps will likewise vary.

---

[9] World Bank. 2018. The Role of Digital Identification for Healthcare: *The Emerging Use Cases.* Washington, D.C.: World Bank.
[10] UNAIDS. 2014. *Considerations and Guidance for Countries adopting National Health Identifiers.* Geneva: UNAIDS.

MODULE 1
LEGAL, INSTITUTIONAL, AND POLITICAL FRAMEWORK

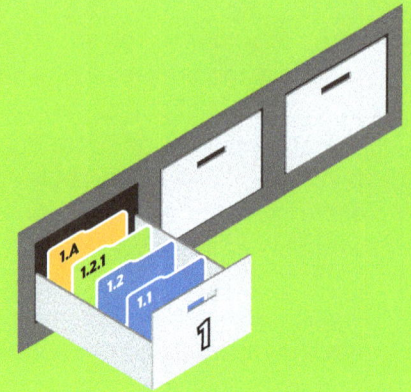

This part of the tool kit aims to retrieve information on the legal, institutional, and political framework. These frameworks are important conditions to build robust, secure, and well-functioning unique identification in the health sector. The institutional setting contributes to well-managed and coordinated implementation of a unique health identifier for health purposes. Laws and regulations on data privacy and protection that regulate how state institutions may use data are required and need to be adapted to the age of electronic storage and ICT usage. They are important conditions to protect individuals from inappropriate privacy intrusion, data misuse, and discriminatory practices. Institutional checks and balances are important accountability and monitoring mechanisms of institutions involved in unique identification.

Figure 5: Legal, Institutional, and Political Framework

1.1 Legal and Policy Framework

Module 1.1. assesses the existing legal and policy framework for unique identification that supports access to health care services. It includes questions on the legal framework on data privacy.

1.2 Stakeholder Mapping

Module 1.2. is a stakeholder mapping that aims to map institutions involved in registration and identification. It further analyzes coordination mechanisms between these different institutions.

1.2.1 Institutional Capacity Assessment

Institutional capacity of individual institutions identified in Module 1.2 can be assessed in Module 1.2.1.

1.A. Donor Support Mapping - Optional

Optional Module 1.A. maps donors active in supporting identification in the health and health-related sectors.

Source: Authors.

1.1

Module 1.1. Legal and Policy Framework

Module 1.1. assesses the existing legal and policy framework for registration and identification that support access to health care services. It includes questions on the legal framework on data privacy.

Laws and regulations on data privacy and protection are important conditions to protect individuals from inappropriate privacy intrusion, data misuse, and discriminatory practices.

ⓗ Health-specific

Patient Registration in Health Facilities	No	In Progress	Law Passed	Enforced Nationwide	Latest Version/ Date
Is there national legislation that makes the electronic registration of patients mandatory in public health facilities?	☐	☐	☐	☐	_____
Is there national legislation that makes the electronic registration of patients mandatory in private health facilities?	☐	☐	☐	☐	_____
Which department within which ministry leads the implementation of the legal framework of patient registration in health facilities?				_____	
List available legislations for patient registration:				_____	
				_____	

Vertical Disease Program Registration	No	In Progress	Law Passed	Enforced Nationwide	Latest Version/ Date
Is there national legislation that specifies the registration of patients within vertical disease programs?	☐	☐	☐	☐	_____
Which department within which ministry leads the implementation of the legal framework of vertical disease programs?				_____	
List available legislations for vertical disease programs				_____	
				_____	

Social Health Protection Enrollment	No	In Progress	Law Passed	Enforced Nationwide	Latest Version/ Date
Is there a national regulation available that specifies the member registration of public health protection agencies (e.g., social health insurance funds)?	☐	☐	☐	☐	_____
Is there a regulation for the private insurance sector?	☐	☐	☐	☐	_____
Which department within which ministry leads the implementation of the legal framework of social health protection programs?				_____	
List available legislation for social health protection programs.				_____	
				_____	

1.1

(hr) Health-related

Birth Registration

	No	In Progress	Law Passed	Enforced Nationwide	Latest Version/ Date
Is there national legislation that makes it mandatory for families to register newborns?	☐	☐	☐	☐	_____
Are there decrees and/or laws that regulate reporting births?	☐	☐	☐	☐	_____
Please list who is legally required to report births by order of obligation					
Which department within which ministry leads the implementation of the legal framework of newborn registration?					
List available legislation for birth registration					

Civil Registration and Vital Statistics

	No	In Progress	Law Passed	Enforced Nationwide	Latest Version/ Date
Is there national legislation that makes the registration of vital (births and deaths) and civil events (marriage, divorce, adoption) mandatory?	☐	☐	☐	☐	_____
Does the country have regulations that oblige all medical care facilities to report all vital events to the vital statistics system within a given time?	☐	☐	☐	☐	_____
Which department within which ministry leads the implementation of the legal framework of civil registration and vital statistics?					
List available legislation for civil registration and vital statistics					

National Identification System

	No	In Progress	Law Passed	Enforced Nationwide	Latest Version/ Date
Is there national legislation that makes the registration of citizens via a national ID system mandatory?	☐	☐	☐	☐	_____
Is there a policy and/or regulation that makes it necessary to present the national ID card for any health services (incl. access to health insurance programs)?	☐	☐	☐	☐	_____
If yes, please list for which health services and/or programs:					
Which department within which ministry leads the implementation of the legal framework of national ID cards?					
List available legislation for national ID card					

© Crosscutting

Health Data Exchange	No	In Progress	Law Passed	Enforced Nationwide	Latest Version/ Date
Is there a legal framework for regulating data exchange within the health sector?	☐	☐	☐	☐	_____
Is there a digital health strategy (eHealth) in place?	☐	☐	☐	☐	_____
Are there regulations available on what electronic data must be shared with institutions outside the health sector (e.g., for monitoring, evaluation, and statistics)?	☐	☐	☐	☐	_____

List available legislation _____

_____

Are there eHealth standards, based on health policies in place? _____

Who is in charge of defining standards for identification and identifiers in the health sector? _____

Have standards been developed for health identifiers in the country?   ☐ Yes   ☐ No

Personal Data Protection	No	In Progress	Law Passed	Enforced Nationwide	Latest Version/ Date
Is there national legislation on privacy or protection of personal data (collection, storage, access, security)?	☐	☐	☐	☐	_____
Is there any legal framework available that regulates the access to personal data, stored at national institutions?	☐	☐	☐	☐	_____
Is there specific national legislation on privacy/data protection available for health-related data?	☐	☐	☐	☐	_____

Is there a supervisory body within government that monitors compliance with privacy and data protection rules?   ☐ Yes   ☐ No

Are the penalties for violation of the privacy rules clearly established and appropriate?   ☐ Yes   ☐ No

Does the legal framework allow for grievance redress for individuals who claim their privacy was violated?   ☐ Yes   ☐ No

Which ministry leads the implementation of the legal framework of personal data protection? _____

List available legislations _____

_____

Government Digital Strategy	No	In Progress	Law Passed	Enforced Nationwide	Latest Version/ Date
Is there a digital (ICT)/eGovernment strategy in place?	☐	☐	☐	☐	_____

If yes, which ministry leads the implementation of the digital (ICT)/ eGovernment strategy? _____

	No	In Progress	Law Passed	Enforced Nationwide	Latest Version/ Date
Is there a specific legal framework for eGovernment available?	☐	☐	☐	☐	_____

Which department within which ministry leads the implementation of the legal framework of eGovernment? _____

1.1

Anti-Discrimination Law	No	In Progress	Law Passed	Enforced Nationwide	Latest Version/ Date
Is there a legal framework to protect against discrimination based on race, ethnicity, religion, sex, sexual orientation, gender identity, political affiliation, or any other?	☐	☐	☐	☐	☐

Other

Please describe other information relevant to the legal framework

_____

_____

_____

_____

Module 1.2. Stakeholder Mapping

Module 1.2. maps institutions involved in registration and identification. It further maps coordination mechanisms between different institutions.

This section of the tool kit can be valuable for anyone who wants to get an overview of actors important in health and health sector-related registration and identification systems.

The institutional capacity of individual institutions can be assessed in Module 1.2.1. Donors supporting activities with regard to health and health sector-related registration and identification systems can be mapped in the optional Module 1.A.

(h) Health-specific

Please list institutions (e.g., hospitals, health centers, vertical disease programs, insurance agencies etc.) involved in the administration of registries for the following areas:

PATIENT REGISTRIES

Name of Institution	Available Registries and/or Identifiers	Government	Autonomous	Other Status (e. g., private)	Number of Branch Offices
Institution 1 :		☐	☐		
Institution 2 :		☐	☐		
Institution 3 :		☐	☐		
Institution 4 :		☐	☐		

SOCIAL HEALTH INSURANCE

Name of Institution	Target group (e.g., formal sector workers, informal sector, poor, civil servants etc.)	Government	Autonomous	Other Status (e. g., private)	Number of Branch Offices
Institution 1 :		☐	☐		
Institution 2 :		☐	☐		
Institution 3 :		☐	☐		
Institution 4 :		☐	☐		

1.2

VERTICAL DISEASE PROGRAM REGISTRIES

Name of Institution	Available Registries and/or Identifiers	Government	Autonomous	Other Status (e. g., private)	Number of Branch Offices
Institution 1 :		☐	☐		
Institution 2 :		☐	☐		
Institution 3 :		☐	☐		
Institution 4 :		☐	☐		

hr Health-related

Please list institutions involved in the administration of registries for the following area:

CRVS SYSTEM/NATIONAL ID SYSTEM/POPULATION REGISTRY

Name of Institution	Available Registries and/or Identifiers	Government (e.g., Ministry)	Autonomous (e.g., national ID Institution)	Other Status (e.g., private)	Number of Branch Offices
Institution 1 :		☐	☐		
Institution 2 :		☐	☐		
Institution 3 :		☐	☐		
Institution 4 :		☐	☐		

c Crosscutting

COORDINATION BETWEEN ACTORS

Steering Committee

Is there a coordinating body or steering committee involving different line ministries, government agencies, and nongovernment stakeholders that focuses on improving coordination of identification-related activities across various sectors and national programs?   ☐ Yes   ☐ No

Please list members _____

_____

How often does the body or committee meet? _____

If available, please attach terms of reference

OUTREACH/COMMUNICATION

National Strategy

Is there a national strategy for communication and awareness for the following identification and/or registration systems in place?

	Periodic	Permanent Process	Customized to Specific Groups
a. National identification system	☐	☐	☐
b. Patient registration in health facilities	☐	☐	☐
c. Birth certificates and/or registration	☐	☐	☐
d. Immunization	☐	☐	☐
e. Social health protection registration	☐	☐	☐
f. Vertical disease management programs (HIV, malaria, tuberculosis)	☐	☐	☐
g. Other, please specify			
_____	☐	☐	☐
_____	☐	☐	☐

1.2.1

Module 1.2.1. Institutional Capacity Assessment

This module assesses an individual institution's capacity identified in module 1.2. It can be applied to a ministry, a department, a health facility, or any other actor identified as important for health and health sector-related registration and identification systems. For countries considering introducing a unique health identifier, it also allows assessing the capacity of a particular institution to implement the scheme.

General

Name of the institution and/or department: _____

What is the mandate of the institution and/or department? _____

Does the institution work with any development partners? Please list

_____

_____

_____

Administration

Is the institution centralized or decentralized? _____

Which functions are decentralized? _____

_____

_____

Please list the registries and/or identifiers the institution administers, the responsible department or division and since when they have been administering the registry and/or identifier.

	Responsible Department/Division	Year
Registry and/or Identifier 1:		
Registry and/or Identifier 2:		
Registry and/or Identifier 3		

Human Resources

Is there an organizational chart? ☐ Yes   ☐ No

If yes, please attach.

1.2.1

How many employees are responsible for administering the registry and/or identifier? _____

Regular training is offered with regard to:

☐ Membership registration or enrollment processes

☐ Customer service

☐ Complaint management

☐ Data privacy and security

Are there capacity development plans available for identification-related activities, data privacy, and security?

_____

_____

_____

Does this ministry, department, or agency have adequate technical expertise to manage an electronic system which allows clear member identification (e.g., member enrollment, updates of member information)?

☐ Yes   ☐ No

If no, which functions, or group of activities lack the required technical expertise?

_____

_____

_____

What kinds of training are needed to administer or manage these activities?

_____

_____

_____

Are there any guidelines that regulate usage of or access to the database? Please list.

_____

_____

_____

Are roles for data managers, data stewards and/or security officers clearly defined and employed?

☐ Yes   ☐ No

Financial Capacity

What is the annual budget of the ministry, department, agency, or program? _____

What is the annual budget to run the registry? _____

Does the ministry, department, or agency allocate revenue within its annual budget for training activities?

☐ Yes   ☐ No

If yes, please list the activities that receive funding.

_____

_____

_____

Does the ministry, department, or agency require external funding for training activities?

☐ Yes   ☐ No

If yes, please state the specific activities which require funding.

_____

_____

_____

Information and Communication Technology

Does this ministry, department, or agency have adequate technical infrastructure (hardware, software, network) to administer or manage registration and/or identity management?

☐ Yes   ☐ No

If no, which areas need support?

_____

_____

_____

1.A

Module 1.A. Donor Support Mapping – Optional

1.A

The optional Module 1.A. maps donors supporting activities in health sector and health sector-related registration and identification systems.

(h) Health-specific

Name the national and/or international donors that support	National	International
Patient registration in health facilities	☐	☐
Donor 1:	☐	☐
Donor 2:	☐	☐
Donor 3:	☐	☐
Donor 4:	☐	☐
Social health protection registry	☐	☐
Donor 1:	☐	☐
Donor 2:	☐	☐
Donor 3:	☐	☐
Donor 4:	☐	☐
Vertical disease program registry	☐	☐
Donor 1:	☐	☐
Donor 2:	☐	☐
Donor 3:	☐	☐
Donor 4:	☐	☐

(hr) Health-related

Name the national and/or international donors that support	National	International
National strategy for citizen identification	☐	☐
Donor 1:	☐	☐
Donor 2:	☐	☐
Donor 3:	☐	☐
Donor 4:	☐	☐

1.A

	National	International
National ID system development and/or implementation	☐	☐
Donor 1:	☐	☐
Donor 2:	☐	☐
Donor 3:	☐	☐
Donor 4:	☐	☐
CRVS system development	☐	☐
Donor 1:	☐	☐
Donor 2:	☐	☐
Donor 3:	☐	☐
Donor 4:	☐	☐
Birth certificates	☐	☐
Donor 1:	☐	☐
Donor 2:	☐	☐
Donor 3:	☐	☐
Donor 4:	☐	☐

ⓒ Crosscutting

Name the national and/or international donors that support	National	International
Data exchange within the health sector	☐	☐
Donor 1:	☐	☐
Donor 2:	☐	☐
Donor 3:	☐	☐
Donor 4:	☐	☐
Personal data protection	☐	☐
Donor 1:	☐	☐
Donor 2:	☐	☐
Donor 3:	☐	☐
Donor 4:	☐	☐
eGovernment	☐	☐
Donor 1:	☐	☐
Donor 2:	☐	☐
Donor 3:	☐	☐
Donor 4:	☐	☐

MODULE 2
ICT INFRASTRUCTURE

This chapter provides an overview on the general usage of ICT and maps to which extent ICT has been introduced for different health and health sector-related registration and identification systems.

Figure 6: Information and Communication Technology Infrastructure

2.1 General ICT usage for identification	Module 2.1. maps the available network structure in the country. More details on available ICT infrastructure relevant for particular identification systems will be assessed in chapter 3.

Source: Authors.

2.1 Module 2.1. General ICT Usage for Identification

Module 2.1. provides an overview on the general usage of ICT and maps to which extent ICT has been introduced for different health and health sector-related registration and identification systems. It further maps the available network structure in the country.

Details on available ICT infrastructure relevant for particular identification systems will be assessed in chapter 3.

h Health-specific

Level of Implementation	Completely (80%-100%)	Partially (< 80%)	Planned	No/Not Planned
To what extent has ICT in your country been introduced for the administration of				
Patient registration in health facilities	☐	☐	☐	☐
Social health protection registration	☐	☐	☐	☐
Vertical disease program registration	☐	☐	☐	☐
Immunization registration	☐	☐	☐	☐

Administrative Level	Central Level	Regional	Local	Not Introduced
If ICT has been introduced, at which administrative level?				
Patient registration in health facilities	☐	☐	☐	☐
Social health protection registration	☐	☐	☐	☐
Vertical disease program registration	☐	☐	☐	☐
Immunization registration	☐	☐	☐	☐

hr Health-related

Level of Implementation	Completely (80%-100%)	Partially (< 80%)	Planned	No/Not Planned
To what extent has ICT in your country been introduced for the administration of				
National ID system	☐	☐	☐	☐
CRVS system	☐	☐	☐	☐
Birth registration	☐	☐	☐	☐
Family registration	☐	☐	☐	☐
Poor household registration	☐	☐	☐	☐

Administrative Level	Central Level	Regional	Local	Not Introduced
If ICT has been introduced, at which administrative level?				
National ID system	☐	☐	☐	☐
CRVS system	☐	☐	☐	☐
Birth registration	☐	☐	☐	☐
Family registration	☐	☐	☐	☐
Poor household registration	☐	☐	☐	☐

ⓒ Crosscutting

Network Structure	Very good	Good	Acceptable	Poor
How would you rate the availability of the 3G network across the country?	☐	☐	☐	☐
How would you rate the availability of intranets within government organizations?	☐	☐	☐	☐
How would you rate the availability of intranets within hospital networks?	☐	☐	☐	☐
How would you rate the power backup in your country (no electricity cuts)?	☐	☐	☐	☐
How would you assess the data recovery handling in case of a natural disaster (risk of data loss)?	☐	☐	☐	☐
Does the approach to managing confidential or sensitive information conform with ISO 27001?	☐	☐	☐	☐

MODULE 3
HEALTH SECTOR AND HEALTH-RELATED REGISTRIES AND IDENTIFIERS

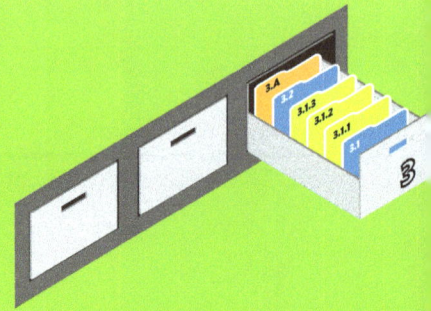

This part collects information about the administrative, operational, and technological aspects of different registration and identification systems in the health and health-related sectors.

Figure 7: Health Sector and Health-Related Registries and Identifiers

3.1 Overview of health sector registries and identifiers	Module 3.1. gives an overview of health sector registries and identifiers. Information about the administration and technical details of different registries and identifiers in the health sector can be assessed in the attached modules (3.1.1.-3.1.3.).
3.1.1. Patient registries in health facilities and health programs	Module 3.1.1. covers patient registries and identifiers for health programs, health facilities, as well as vertical disease programs.
3.1.2. Membership databases and identifiers	Module 3.1.2. covers registries and identifiers for various health insurance and other social protection schemes.
3.1.3. Immunization registries	Module 3.1.3. assesses immunization registries.
3.2. Overview of health-related registries and identifiers	Module 3.2. covers registration and identification systems beyond the health sector including national identification and CRVS.
3.A. Quick review of existing identifiers - optional	Optional module 3.A. allows for a quick scan of the different identifiers.

Source: Authors.

3.1

Module 3.1. Overview of Health Sector Registries and Identifiers

3.1

Module 3.1. gives an overview of health sector registries and identifiers. Information about the administration and technical details of different registries and identifiers in the health sector can be assessed in the attached modules (3.1.1.-3.1.3.). Module 3.1.1. covers patient registries and identifiers for health programs, health facilities, as well as vertical disease programs. Module 3.1.2. covers registries and identifiers for various health insurance and other social protection schemes. Module 3.1.3. assesses immunization registries.

(h) Health-specific

Patient Registries	Yes	No
Does a unified electronic centralized patient registry exist?	☐	☐

If no, how would you best describe the existing registries in the country (multiple answers possible)?

☐ Each facility or hospital has their own registry. Registries are not interconnected.
☐ Each facility or hospital has their own registry. Registries are interconnected.
☐ Several health programs (e.g. malaria program, immunization registry) have their own registry

If applicable, please list health programs and/or departments that use their own registries, e.g., maternal and family health (except vertical disease programs, which will be covered below):

_____

_____

	Yes	No
Are patient identifiers issued in the country?	☐	☐

If yes, how could you best describe the patient identification situation in the country (multiple answers possible)?

☐ There is a unique patient identifier
☐ Different health programs have different identifiers
☐ Different health facility or hospital have their own identifier
☐ Clusters of health facility or hospital have a common identifier

If applicable, please list health programs that use their own identifiers (except vertical disease programs):

_____

_____

_____

Vertical Disease Program Registries	Yes	No
Is there a unified registry for people living with HIV available?	☐	☐
Is there a unified registry for malaria patients available?	☐	☐
Is there a unified registry for tuberculosis patients available?	☐	☐

Immunization Registry	Yes	No
Is there a unified registry for immunization available?	☐	☐

Social Health Protection Registries	Yes	No
Are there registries for social health protection available?	☐	☐

If yes, how would you best describe the situation in your country?

☐ A unified social security number exists

☐ A unified health insurance number exists

☐ Different health insurance schemes use their own member identifier

Please list the health insurance schemes in the country by group

Civil servants

_____

_____

_____

Formal sector

_____

_____

_____

Informal sector (nonpoor)

_____

_____

_____

Informal sector (poor)

_____

_____

_____

Other groups

_____

_____

_____

Module 3.1.1. Patient Registries in Health Facilities and Health Programs

This module assesses a particular patient registry and identifiers either at a particular health facility, a cluster of facilities, or for a particular health program (e.g., maternal, newborn, and child health). The questionnaire can be repeated for each facility, cluster, or health program selected to be assessed. It does not cover registration of members for insurance schemes. For the insurance schemes, please refer to Module 3.1.2.

ⓗ Health-specific

General

Applicable to (pick one)
☐ Health facility   ☐ Health program
☐ Cluster of facilities   ☐ Vertical disease program

Disease program, if applicable: ☐ HIV   ☐ Malaria   ☐ Tuberculosis

Name of health program, if applicable: _____

Administration

Which institution/s is/are responsible for the administration of this registry? _____

At which level is data stored?	Personalized data	Aggregate data	No data
National	☐	☐	☐
Provincial	☐	☐	☐
District	☐	☐	☐
Commune or municipal	☐	☐	☐

How many health facilities does this registry cover? _____

Is the database interoperable or linked with other registries?   ☐ Yes   ☐ No

If yes, please list:

_____

_____

_____

Who can access this database?	All data	Some data	Please specify
a. Medical staff:	☐	☐	_____
b. Administrative staff:	☐	☐	_____
c. Patients:	☐	☐	_____
d. Others, please specify:			
_____	☐	☐	_____
_____	☐	☐	_____

Registration

What percentage of the entire population does the registry cover?	☐ <40%	☐ 40%-80%	☐ >80%
Who is covered?	☐ Citizens only	☐ Citizens and residents	☐ Citizens, residents, and others, please specify: _____
Where or how is patient registration carried out?	☐ At health facilities	☐ Through health worker community/ household visits	☐ Other, please specify _____

	Yes	No	Please specify
Are there adequate numbers of registration points to cover the whole country?	☐	☐	_____
Do patient registrars have adequate equipment to carry out their functions (e.g., forms, telephones, photocopiers, computers, tablets)?	☐	☐	_____
Who carries out the registration (e.g., government official, contractor, nurse, doctor, community health worker)?			_____
Have they received training to carry out their functions?	☐	☐	_____

What documents are required to register?

☐ No documents

☐ National ID card

☐ Health insurance ID card (if member)

☐ Birth certificate

☐ Family book

☐ Civil servant ID card

☐ Worker ID card

☐ Other, please specify

_____

_____

What general information is captured in the registry?	Yes	No	Mandatory
a. Name	☐	☐	☐
b. Date of birth	☐	☐	☐
c. Sex	☐	☐	☐
d. Address	☐	☐	☐
e. Information on family members	☐	☐	☐
f. Citizenship	☐	☐	☐
g. Patient ID number	☐	☐	☐

	Yes	No	Mandatory
h. National ID number	☐	☐	☐
i. Passport number	☐	☐	☐
j. Health insurance ID number	☐	☐	☐
k. Birth certificate number	☐	☐	☐
l. Family book ID number	☐	☐	☐
m. Driving license ID number	☐	☐	☐
n. Other, please specify			
_____	☐	☐	☐
_____	☐	☐	☐

ICT	Paper-Based Only	Electronic	Mixed	Electronic Planned
At which level is electronic registration of patients available?				
National	☐	☐	☐	☐
Provincial	☐	☐	☐	☐
District	☐	☐	☐	☐
Other, please specify	☐	☐	☐	☐

Is software in use for operational procedures?   ☐ Yes   ☐ No

If yes, which software programs are in use at health facilities or programs and what are the core functions?

Core Functions: Name of software solution(s)

☐ Patient registration   _____

☐ Creation of ID numbers   _____

☐ Patient card issuance   _____

☐ Biometric data capture   _____

☐ Transaction with health insurance funds   _____

☐ Establishment of medical records   _____

☐ Transactions to or from other health programs   _____

☐ Billing   _____

☐ Statistics   _____

Biometrics	Yes	No	Mandatory
What biometric information is captured in the registry?			
a. None	☐	☐	☐
b. Digital facial image	☐	☐	☐
c. Fingerprints	☐	☐	☐
d. Iris	☐	☐	☐
e. Other, please specify			
_____	☐	☐	☐
_____	☐	☐	☐
Are readers for authentication purposes are available in all locations?	☐	☐	

ID Number	Yes	No
Does the registry issue its own identifier (identification number)?	☐	☐
Is there a central assigning authority for the patient ID number in place?	☐	☐
If yes, please name:		
Is a new identifier request initiated by an authorized local person (e.g., by patient, a clinician, or an administrator)?	☐	☐
How many patient ID numbers were issued last year?		
How many patient ID numbers have been issued to date (cumulative figure)?		
What happens with an ID number in case of decease of a registered person/ID holder?		
Does the identifier consist of alphanumeric characters that do not represent any aspect of the identity of an individual person (e.g., date of birth, place of residence)?	☐	☐
Does the identifier contain any information about the health facility or program (e.g., location, year started)?	☐	☐
Does the number allow cross-referencing to other numbers (e.g., National ID number)?	☐	☐
Can the number be merged to consolidate multiple identifiers that belong to the same individual?	☐	☐
Can the number be split to assign new identifiers to two or more individuals who have been assigned a single identifier in error?	☐	☐
Can the number be linked to health records in both manual and automated environments?	☐	☐
Is the identifier deployable in a variety of technologies, such as scanners and barcode readers?	☐	☐
Can clinical data be linked retroactively to a unique identifier (in cases where medical data got collected before the implementation of an ID number)?	☐	☐

ID Card

What kind of ID card is issued?

☐ None

☐ Paper

☐ Plastic

☐ Barcode

☐ Magnetic strip

☐ Smart card

If Smartcard:

Is there a chip on the card?	☐ Yes	☐ No
What other information is stored on the card?		
Are biometrics stored on the card?	☐ Yes	☐ No

What external security features are on the card?

- ☐ Holograms
- ☐ Microprinting
- ☐ UV printing
- ☐ Other, please specify

_____

_____

Will the card be replaced if it is lost?

- ☐ Yes, with a fee
- ☐ Yes, without fee
- ☐ No

What are the production costs associated to issuing the patient ID document?

1. _____
2. _____
3. _____
4. _____

How long does it take to issue a patient ID document from the time of registration (number of days)?

_____

Are there specific population groups that encounter obstacles to obtaining a patient ID document?

- ☐ Indigenous people
- ☐ Migrants and/or nomadic people
- ☐ Poor people
- ☐ Women
- ☐ Persons living with HIV
- ☐ Other, please specify

_____

_____

Module 3.1.2. Membership Databases and Identifiers for Health Insurance and Other Social Protection Schemes

This module collects specific information on registries and identifiers for members of health insurance and other social protection schemes. One questionnaire for each insurance scheme is recommended.

General

Which group is this health insurance or social protection scheme for?

☐ Civil servants

☐ Formal sector

☐ Informal sector (nonpoor)

☐ Informal sector (poor)

☐ Other groups

Name of the insurance or social protection scheme: _____

Administration

Name of the health insurance or social protection scheme implementing agency:
_____

Does the agency have a decentralized structure?		☐ Yes	☐ No

If yes, at which level is member data stored?	All data	Aggregate data	No data
National	☐	☐	☐
Provincial	☐	☐	☐
District	☐	☐	☐
Commune or municipal	☐	☐	☐

Is the database linked to other registries?		☐ Yes	☐ No

If yes, please list:

_____

_____

_____

Who can access this database?	All data	Some data	Please specify
a. Health insurance scheme staff	☐	☐	_____
b. Administrative staff at health facility	☐	☐	_____
c. Members	☐	☐	_____
d. Others, please specify			
_____	☐	☐	_____
_____	☐	☐	_____

Enrollment

At what age can a person become a member?	_____		

What percentage of the entire population does the database cover?	☐ <40%	☐ 40%–80%	☐ >80%
Who is covered?	☐ Citizens only	☐ Citizens and residents	☐ Citizens, residents and others, please specify: _____
Where or how is enrollment carried out?	☐ At health facilities (e.g., hospital staff)	☐ Through health insurance staff	☐ Other, please specify _____

	Yes	No	Please specify
Are the adequate enrollment points to cover the whole country?	☐	☐	_____
Have personnel carrying out enrollment received training to perform their functions?	☐	☐	_____

What documents are required for enrollment?

☐ No documents

☐ National ID card

☐ Birth certificate

☐ Family book

☐ Civil servant ID card

☐ Worker ID card

☐ Work permit

☐ ID poor card

☐ Other, please specify

_____

_____

What general information is captured in the health insurance membership database?	Yes	No	Mandatory
a. Name	☐	☐	☐
b. Date of birth	☐	☐	☐
c. Sex	☐	☐	☐
d. Address	☐	☐	☐
e. Information on family members	☐	☐	☐
f. Patient ID number	☐	☐	☐
g. National ID number	☐	☐	☐
h. Passport number	☐	☐	☐
i. Health insurance ID number	☐	☐	☐

	Yes	No	Mandatory
j. Birth certificate ID number	☐	☐	☐
k. Family book ID number	☐	☐	☐
l. Driving license ID number	☐	☐	☐
m. Other, please specify			
_____	☐	☐	☐
_____	☐	☐	☐

Information and Communication Technology	Yes	No
Is software in use for operational procedures?	☐	☐

If yes, which software programs are in use and what are the core functions?

Core Functions	Name of software program
☐ Membership registration	_____
☐ Creation of ID numbers	_____
☐ Membership card issuance	_____
☐ Biometric data capture	_____
☐ Transactions with health facilities	_____
☐ Contribution collection	_____
☐ Provider reimbursement	_____
☐ Transactions to or from other health programs	_____
☐ Billing	_____
☐ Statistics	_____

Biometrics	Yes	No	Mandatory
What biometric information is captured in the membership database?			
a. None	☐	☐	☐
b. Digital facial image	☐	☐	☐
c. Fingerprints	☐	☐	☐
d. Iris	☐	☐	☐
e. Other, please specify			
_____	☐	☐	☐
_____	☐	☐	☐
Are readers for authentication purposes available in all locations?	☐	☐	

ID Number	Yes	No
Does the registry issue its own identifier (health insurance or social protection ID number)?	☐	☐

If yes, please answer the questions below.
Is there a central assigning authority for the member ID number in place? ☐ ☐

If yes, please name: _____

How many ID numbers were issued last year? _____

How many ID numbers have been issued to date (cumulative figure)? _____

What happens with an ID number in case of decease of a registered member? _____

Does the identifier consist of alphanumeric characters that do not represent any aspect of the identity of an individual person (e.g., date of birth, place of residence)? ☐ ☐

Does the number allow crossreferencing to other numbers? (e.g., National ID number) ☐ ☐

Can the number be merged to consolidate multiple identifiers that belong to the same individual? ☐ ☐

Can the number be split to assign new identifiers to two or more individuals who have been assigned a single identifier in error? ☐ ☐

Can the number be linked to patient registration systems in hospitals or health centers? ☐ ☐

ID Card

What kind of ID card is issued?

    ☐ None

    ☐ Paper

    ☐ Plastic

    ☐ Barcode

    ☐ Magnetic strip

    ☐ Smart card

If Smartcard:
  Is there a chip on the card? ☐ Yes ☐ No

  Are biometrics stored on the card? ☐ Yes ☐ No

What external security features are on the card?

    ☐ Holograms

    ☐ Microprinting

    ☐ UV printing

    ☐ Other, please specify

_____

_____

What are the production costs associated with issuing the membership ID document?

1. _____
2. _____
3. _____
4. _____
5. _____

What are the costs for the patient for getting a membership ID document?

_____

Is the health insurance ID card commonly used for any of the following purposes?

☐ Obtaining public health services

☐ Obtaining private services

☐ Enrolling in other social insurance programs

☐ Qualifying for cash transfers, food, or other safety net programs

☐ Other, please specify

_____

_____

Module 3.1.3. Immunization Registries

This module assesses a particular immunization registry either at a particular health facility, a cluster of facilities, or for a particular health program. The questionnaire can be repeated as often as necessary for each facility, cluster, or health program.

General

Applicable to	☐ Health facility/ies	☐ Health program

Name of health program, if applicable: _____

Disease program, if applicable:	☐ HIV	☐ Malaria	☐ TB

Administration

Which institution/s is/are responsible for the administration of this registry? _____

At which level is data stored?	Personalized data	Aggregate data	No data
National	☐	☐	☐
Provincial	☐	☐	☐
District	☐	☐	☐
Commune or municipal	☐	☐	☐

In how many facilities are immunization records recorded? _____

Is the database linked to other registries?	☐ Yes	☐ No

If yes, please list:

_____

_____

_____

Who can access this registry?	All Data	Some Data	Please specify
a. Medical staff:	☐	☐	_____
b. Administrative staff:	☐	☐	_____
c. Patients:	☐	☐	_____
d. Others, please specify:			
_____	☐	☐	_____
_____	☐	☐	_____

Registration

What percentage of the entire population does the registry cover?	☐ < 40%	☐ 40%-80%	☐ >80%
Who is covered?	☐ Citizens only	☐ Citizens and residents	☐ Citizens, residents and others, please specify: _____
Where or how is immunization registration carried out?	☐ at health facilities	☐ through health worker community/ household visits	☐ Other, please specify _____

	Yes	No	Please specify:
Are there adequate numbers of immunization points to cover the whole country?	☐	☐	_____
Do patient registrars have adequate equipment to carry out their functions (for example, forms, telephones, photocopiers, computers, tablets)?	☐	☐	_____
Who carries out the registration (e.g., government official, contractor, nurse, doctor, community health worker)?			_____
Have they received training to carry out their functions?	☐	☐	_____

What documents are required to register?

☐ No documents

☐ National ID card

☐ Health insurance ID card (if member)

☐ Birth certificate

☐ Family book

☐ Other, please specify

_____

_____

Which of the following information is captured in the registry?	Yes	No	Mandatory
a. Name	☐	☐	☐
b. Date of birth	☐	☐	☐
c. Sex	☐	☐	☐
d. Address	☐	☐	☐
e. Information on family members	☐	☐	☐
f. Citizenship	☐	☐	☐
g. Patient ID number	☐	☐	☐

	Yes	No	Mandatory
h. National ID number	☐	☐	☐
j. Health insurance ID number	☐	☐	☐
k. Birth certificate ID number	☐	☐	☐
l. Family book ID number	☐	☐	☐
n. Other, please specify			
_____	☐	☐	☐
_____	☐	☐	☐

ICT	Paper-Based Only	Electronic	Mixed	Electronic Planned
At which level is electronic registration of immunization records available?				
National	☐	☐	☐	☐
Provincial	☐	☐	☐	☐
District	☐	☐	☐	☐
Commune or municipal	☐	☐	☐	☐

Is software in use for operational procedures?   ☐ Yes   ☐ No

If yes, which software programs are in use at health facilities or programs and what are the core functions?

Core Functions: Name of software program(s)

☐ Patient registration   _____

☐ Creation of ID numbers   _____

☐ Immunization card issuance   _____

☐ Biometric data capture   _____

☐ Transactions with health insurance funds _____

☐ Creation of medical records   _____

☐ Transactions to/from other health programs _____

☐ Billing   _____

Biometrics	Yes	No	Mandatory
What biometric information is captured in the registry?			
a. None	☐	☐	☐
b. Digital facial image	☐	☐	☐
c. Fingerprints	☐	☐	☐
d. Iris	☐	☐	☐
e. Other, please specify			
_____	☐	☐	☐
_____	☐	☐	☐
Are readers for authentication purposes are available in all locations?	☐	☐	

ID Number	Yes	No
Does the immunization registry issue its own identifier (identification number)?	☐	☐
Is there a central assigning authority for the ID number in place?	☐	☐
If yes, please name: _____		
Is a new identifier request initiated by an authorized local person? (e.g., by patient, a clinician, or an administrator)	☐	☐
How many ID numbers were issued last year? _____		
How many ID numbers have been issued to date (cumulative figure)? _____		

ID card or immunization card

What kind of ID card is issued?

☐ None

☐ Paper

☐ Plastic

☐ Barcode

☐ Magnetic strip

☐ Smart card

What are the production costs associated with the issuing the immunization ID document?

1. _____

2. _____

3. _____

4. _____

What are the costs for the patient for getting a membership ID document?

1. _____

2. _____

3. _____

4. _____

How long does it take to issue an immunization ID document from the time of registration (number of days)? _____

Are there specific population groups that encounter obstacles to obtaining a patient ID document?

☐ Indigenous people

☐ Migrants and/or nomadic people

☐ Poor people

☐ Women

☐ Persons living with HIV

☐ Other, please specify

_____

_____

Module 3.2. Overview of Health-Related Registries

3.2

This section gives an overview of all registries and identifiers related to the health sector. The section covers national identification systems, birth registration and certificates, and the CRVS system.

hr Health-related

NATIONAL ID SYSTEM	Yes	No
Is a national ID number or card available?	☐	☐

Administration	Yes	No
Which institution is in charge of national identifiers?	_____	
Is there a separate database for national identifiers?	☐	☐
Does the institution have a decentralized structure?	☐	☐

At which level is data stored?	Personalized data	Aggregate data	No data
National	☐	☐	☐
Province	☐	☐	☐
District	☐	☐	☐
Commune or municipal	☐	☐	☐

Is the database linked to other registries? ☐ Yes ☐ No

If yes, please list:

_____

_____

_____

_____

Who can access this database?	All Data	Some Data	Please specify
a. Only staff of the institution	☐	☐	_____
b. Only selected staff of the institution	☐	☐	_____
c. All officials across government agencies	☐	☐	_____
d. Other agencies, accredited by the government (e.g., semi-autonomous bodies, health insurance agencies)	☐	☐	_____
e. Others, please specify			
_____	☐	☐	_____
_____	☐	☐	_____

3.2

Registration

| What percentage of the entire population does the national ID database cover? | ☐ <40% | ☐ 40%-80% | ☐ >80% |

Is the national ID number intended to cover

☐ All residents

☐ All citizens

☐ All adult citizens

☐ Other, please specify

_____

_____

At what age can a person obtain an ID number? _____

| Where or how is registration or application carried out? | ☐ Automatically issued at birth after receiving the birth certificate | ☐ Registration at municipal offices | ☐ Other, please specify _____ |

	Yes	No	Please specify:
Are there adequate numbers of registration points to cover the whole country?	☐	☐	_____
Do offices issuing national ID numbers have adequate equipment to carry out their functions (e.g., forms, telephones, photocopiers, and computers)?	☐	☐	_____
Have officials received training to carry out their functions?	☐	☐	_____

What documents are required to register?

☐ No documents

☐ Birth registration document

☐ Birth certificate

☐ Community/village chief verification

☐ Verification of other individuals

☐ Other, please specify

_____

_____

What information is captured in the national ID database?

☐ Name

☐ Date of birth

☐ Sex

☐ Address

☐ Ethnicity

☐ Religion

☐ Political affiliation

☐ Information on parents or other family members

☐ Other, please specify

_____

_____

Is a photo captured at the time of registration?   ☐ Yes   ☐ No

ICT

Is the ID database digitized or stored electronically?			☐ Yes	☐ No

At which level is electronic registration available?	Paper-Based Only	Electronic	Mixed	Electronic Planned
National	☐	☐	☐	☐
Provincial	☐	☐	☐	☐
District	☐	☐	☐	☐
Commune or municipal	☐	☐	☐	☐

Is software in use for operational procedures?   ☐ Yes   ☐ No

If yes, which programs are in use and what are the core functions?

Core Functions: Name of software solution(s)

☐ Registration _____

☐ Creation of ID numbers _____

☐ National ID card issuance _____

☐ Biometric data capture _____

☐ Transactions with government agencies _____

Biometrics

What biometric information is captured during registration?

☐ None

☐ Digital facial image

☐ Fingerprints

☐ Iris

☐ Other, please specify

_____

_____

Are biometrics stored on a central server?   ☐ Yes   ☐ No

If yes, please list who has access to the biometrics database
(e. g., government departments or agencies, private institutions)?

_____

_____

3.2

What biometric capturing devices are in use? (e.g., fingerprint readers)	Central Level	Regional	Local	Not Introduced
1. _____	☐	☐	☐	☐
2. _____	☐	☐	☐	☐
3. _____	☐	☐	☐	☐
4. _____	☐	☐	☐	☐
5. _____	☐	☐	☐	☐
6. _____	☐	☐	☐	☐
7. _____	☐	☐	☐	☐

ID Number

How long is the national ID number valid?	☐ Lifelong	☐ Change after card expiry	☐ Other, please specify _____ _____

Is there a central assigning authority for the national ID number in place?	☐ Yes	☐ No

If yes, please name:

_____

How many ID numbers were issued last year? _____

How many ID numbers have been issued to date (cumulative figure)? _____

What happens with an ID number in case of death of a registered person? _____

	Yes	No
Does the identifier consist of alphanumeric characters that do not represent any aspect of the identity of an individual person (e.g., date of birth, place of residence)?	☐	☐
Does the number allow cross-referencing to other numbers? (e.g., passport number)	☐	☐
Can the number be merged to consolidate multiple identifiers that belong to the same individual?	☐	☐
Can the number be split to assign new identifiers to two or more individuals who have been assigned a single identifier in error?	☐	☐

National ID Card

What kind of ID card is issued?

☐ None

☐ Paper

☐ Plastic

☐ Barcode

☐ Magnetic strip

☐ Smart card

If Smartcard, is there a chip on the card?   ☐ Yes   ☐ No

If yes:

What is the capacity of the chip?   _____

What information does the chip hold?   _____

What information is used for authentication?   _____

What information is stored on the card and
who has access to it?   _____

What external security features are on the card?

    ☐ Holograms

    ☐ Microprinting

    ☐ UV printing

    ☐ Other, please specify

_____

_____

What information is printed on the face of the card?	What information is not printed on the ID card but machine readable?
☐ ID number	☐ ID number
☐ Name	☐ Name
☐ Address	☐ Address
☐ Age	☐ Age
☐ Sex	☐ Sex
☐ Ethnicity	☐ Ethnicity
☐ Political affiliation	☐ Political affiliation
☐ Religion	☐ Religion
☐ Other, please specify	☐ Other, please specify

At what age can a person obtain an ID card?_____

What is the validity of the national ID card? How often must the card be replaced?

    ☐ Never

    ☐ Less than every 3 years

    ☐ Less than every 5 years

    ☐ Less than every 10 years

What are the costs for a person for getting a national ID card?_____

Does a person need to pay for replacement of a lost card?   ☐ Yes   ☐ No

Is the national ID number or card commonly used for any of the following purposes?

    ☐ Obtaining public health services

    ☐ Obtaining private services

    ☐ Enrolling in social insurance programs

    ☐ Qualifying for cash transfers, food or other safety net programs

    ☐ Other, please specify

_____

_____

CRVS SYSTEM

Administration

Which institution is responsible for administering the civil registry? _____

Does the institution have a decentralized structure?   ☐ Yes   ☐ No

At which level is data stored?	Personalized Data	Aggregate Data	No Data
National	☐	☐	☐
Provincial	☐	☐	☐
District	☐	☐	☐
Commune or municipal	☐	☐	☐

How are birth and death records transmitted from local and regional offices to a central storage in the capital city?

_____

Which institution is responsible for administering vital statistics? _____

Can the vital statistics system generate both national and subnational statistics on births and deaths each year?   ☐ Yes   ☐ No

Is the civil registry database linked to other registries in the health sector?   ☐ Yes   ☐ No

If yes, please list

_____

_____

_____

Has a CRVS rapid assessment been carried out?   ☐ Yes   ☐ No

Birth registration

What percentage of the entire population does the civil registry cover?	☐ <40%	☐ 40%-80%	☐ >80%
If separate, what percentage of the entire population does the birth registry cover?	☐ <40%	☐ 40%-80%	☐ >80%
According to the most recent evaluation, how complete (in percentage) is birth registration in your country?	_____		

Who is responsible to register a birth? _____

Who is responsible to notify a birth (e.g., parents, doctors, nurse)? _____

Where/how is birth registration carried out?

☐ at health facilities   ☐ through health worker community/ household visits   ☐ Other, please specify _____

	Yes	No	Please specify:
Does the institution responsible for birth registration have adequate equipment to carry out their function (e.g., forms, telephones, photocopiers, and computers)?	☐	☐	_____
Have they received training to carry out their functions?	☐	☐	_____
Within how many days must a birth be registered?			_____
Is birth registration free of cost?	☐	☐	_____
Is late registration possible?	☐	☐	_____
If yes, describe the process.			_____
Is there a fine for late registration?	☐	☐	_____
Who pays the fine?			_____

Are there any outreach activities at communities to register births or encourage birth registration? Please describe _____

What documents are required to register a birth?

☐ No documents

☐ Father's national ID card

☐ Mother's national ID card

☐ Family book

☐ Mother's birth certificate

☐ Father's birth certificate

☐ Parent's marriage certificate

☐ Other, please specify

_____

Which of the following information is captured for birth registration	Yes	No	Mandatory
a. Name	☐	☐	☐
b. Date of birth	☐	☐	☐
c. Sex	☐	☐	☐
d. Address	☐	☐	☐
e. Citizenship	☐	☐	☐
f. Information on family members	☐	☐	☐
g. Father's name	☐	☐	☐

h. Mother's name	☐	☐	☐
i. Mother's date of birth	☐	☐	☐
j. Father's date of birth	☐	☐	☐
k. Mother's national ID number	☐	☐	☐
l. Father's national ID number	☐	☐	☐
m. Family book ID number	☐	☐	☐
n. Other, please specify			
_____	☐	☐	☐
_____	☐	☐	☐

How are birth registries linked to the health sector?

☐ They are not linked to the health sector.

☐ Birth registrations are regularly reported to the ministry of health.

☐ Birth registration is regularly communicated to public health insurance institutions.

What is the estimated percentage of births that take place in medical facilities (i.e., institutional births)?

_____

Do medical facilities automatically notify civil registration offices or local authorities of births? Please specify.

_____

Are there specific population groups not/inadequately covered in CRVS?

☐ Indigenous people

☐ Migrants and/or nomadic people

☐ Poor people

☐ Women

Death Registration

According to the most recent evaluation, how complete (in percentage) is death registration in your country?

_____

How are death registries linked to the health sector?

☐ They are not linked to the health sector

☐ Death registrations are regularly reported to the ministry of health.

☐ Death registration is regularly communicated to public health insurance institutions

What is the estimated percentage of deaths that take place in medical facilities (i.e., institutional deaths not births)?

_____

Do medical facilities automatically notify civil registration offices or local authorities of deaths in facilities? Please specify.

_____

	Yes	No
Does the country use the standard international form of medical certificate of cause of death for reporting?	☐	☐
Do doctors receive training for certifying the cause of death?	☐	☐

Other Vital Events

Which other vital events are recorded in the civil registry?

☐ Marriage

☐ Divorce

☐ Other, please specify

_____

_____

ICT

At which level are civil registration data digitized, stored electronically?	Paper-Based Only	Electronic	Mixed	Electronic Planned
National	☐	☐	☐	☐
Provincial	☐	☐	☐	☐
District	☐	☐	☐	☐
Commune or municipal	☐	☐	☐	☐

ID Number

	Yes	No
Is a civil registration number issued (which is different from the national ID number)?	☐	☐
Is a birth registration number issued (which is different from the national ID number)?	☐	☐
Is a birth certificate number issued (which is different from the national ID number)?	☐	☐

Birth Certificate

Are there costs for a person associated to getting a birth certificate?	☐ Yes	☐ No

If yes, how much does a birth certificate cost?

_____

Describe the process from the time of birth to the issuance of a birth certificate, including how long it takes (number of days)?

_____

_____

Are there specific population groups that encounter obstacles to obtaining a birth certificate?

☐ Indigenous people

☐ Migrants and/or nomadic people

☐ Poor people

☐ Women

☐ Other, please specify

_____

_____

Is the birth certificate commonly used for any of the following purposes?

☐ Obtaining public health services

☐ Obtaining private health services

☐ Enrolling in social insurance programs

☐ Qualifying for cash transfers, food, or other safety net programs

☐ Other, please specify

_____

_____

3.A

Module 3.A. Quick Review of Existing Identifiers (Identification Numbers) throughout the Country - Optional

What identifiers (ID numbers) exist throughout the country? Use separate lines if more than one identifier exists (e.g., ID numbers for migrants, temporary cards)

Identifier	Number of digits	Example	Unique No.
Citizen identification			
National ID number			
Passport (adult)			
Passport (child)			
Birth certificate number			
Social Protection			
Health Insurance ID number			
Pension ID number			
Other Social Protection ID numbers			
Patient Identification–Health/ Vertical Disease Programs (HIV/TB/Malaria)			
Immunization ID number:			
Other:			

REFERENCES

ADB. 2016. *On the road to universal health coverage: Every person matters.* Manila: ADB. https://www.adb.org/sites/default/files/publication/183512/uhc-every-person-matters.pdf.

Inter Agency Social Protection Assessments Partnership. 2016. *Identification Systems for Social Protection.* Washington, D.C.: World Bank. http://ispatools.org/wp-content/uploads/2017/05/ID-tool.pdf.

Thai Health Information Standards Development Center (THIS)/Health Systems Research Institute (HSRI). 2013. *Review of National Civil Registration and Vital Statistics Systems: A case study of Thailand.* Nonthaburi: THIS. http://www.this.or.th/files/77.pdf.

UNAIDS. 2014. *Consideration and Guidance for Countries Adopting National Health Identifiers. Geneva: UNAIDS/PEPFAR.* http://www.unaids.org/sites/default/files/media_asset/JC2640_nationalhealthidentifiers_en.pdf.

WHO. 2010. *Rapid assessment of national civil registration and vital statistics systems. Geneva: WHO.* http://apps.who.int/iris/bitstream/10665/70470/1/WHO_IER_HSI_STM_2010.1_eng.pdf.

World Bank. 2017. *Principles on Identification for Sustainable Development: Toward the Digital Age.* Washington, D.C.: World Bank. http://documents.worldbank.org/curated/en/213581486378184357/pdf/112614-REVISED-English-ID4D-IdentificationPrinciples.pdf.

———. 2018a. *Guidelines for ID4D Diagnostics.* Washington, D.C.: World Bank. http://pubdocs.worldbank.org/en/370121518449921710/GuidelinesID4DDiagnostic-030618.pdf.

———. 2018b. *The Role of Digital Identification for Healthcare: The Emerging Use Cases.* Washington, D.C.: World Bank. http://pubdocs.worldbank.org/en/595741519657604541/DigitalIdentification-HealthcareReportFinal.pdf.

www.ingramcontent.com/pod-product-compliance
Lightning Source LLC
Chambersburg PA
CBHW041432270326
41935CB00025B/1859